The Global State of Gender Equality: An Overview of Empirical Findings

Gender Equality, Volume 2

Milos Kankaras

Published by Dr. Miloš Kankaraš, 2022.

While every precaution has been taken in the preparation of this book, the publisher assumes no responsibility for errors or omissions, or for damages resulting from the use of the information contained herein.

THE GLOBAL STATE OF GENDER EQUALITY: AN OVERVIEW OF EMPIRICAL FINDINGS

First edition. July 23, 2022.

Copyright © 2022 Milos Kankaras.

ISBN: 979-8223905172

Written by Milos Kankaras.

The Global State of Gender Equality

An Overview of Empirical Fidings

Dr Miloš Kankaraš

Executive summary

The world is still a long way from gender equality. Over and over again, women are given fewer opportunities or are treated worse than men in comparable situations. This inequality spreads across different aspects of women's everyday lives, although it varies across these domains in terms of its severity and characteristics. Moreover, gender equality is markedly different across countries and regions worldwide. For example, of the top 20 ranking countries globally in the UN's SDG Gender Index, 18 are in Europe and North America, and two are in the Pacific region (Australia and New Zealand). Conversely, of the bottom 20 ranking countries, 17 are in Sub-Saharan Africa. So, while some northern-European countries are reaching or even exceeding parity levels across many areas, women in several world regions face incredibly high levels of inequality and even violence and abuse.

Furthermore, although many developed countries achieve relatively high scores on various global gender equality indices, the overall picture at the country level generally tends to hide the severity of the gender gap across the world. That happens because the poorer countries and countries with lower levels of gender equality also tend to be more populous. That leads to a situation where around 80% of the girls and women in the participating sample of 129 countries live in countries that generally "fail" or "barely pass" on gender equality.

Available trend data identify various changes in the levels of gender equality around the world, although their magnitude and direction are not always as expected or desired. On the positive side, the empirical evidence shows that things are changing for the better in several areas of gender equality at the global level. These include markedly better education outcomes for girls and higher levels of political participation. Nevertheless, the progress has generally been painfully slow, and it has occasionally taken a turn for the worse in some areas and regions.

Lack of progress in the area of economic empowerment

Women continue to do most of the unpaid domestic care and work, although this kind of work has intensified for both men and women during the COVID-19 pandemic. Currently, on an average day globally, women spend about two and a half times more doing unpaid care and domestic work than men (4.2 hours compared to 1.7, respectively). What is more, this uneven distribution of unpaid domestic and care work prevents women from participating in the labour market.

As a result, less than 50% of working-age women are in the labour market, which is lower today than twenty years ago (World Bank, 2021; **Appendix 8**). Compared with 74% of employed men, the employment gap is huge and persistent. Moreover, the pandemic is expected to exacerbate these gender disparities. Many women work in the sectors hardest hit by COVID-19 measures, including paid domestic work, hospitality and catering services, and the retail industry.

Few cracks in the glass ceiling

In areas of political and economic power and decision-making, the situation is changing for the better, while in others, it is largely stagnating. But in all of the available indicators, the gap between women and men regarding power access and the ability to participate in decision-making is vast. Women were still holding only 28% of managerial positions globally in 2019, almost the same percentage as in 1995. Only 18% of enterprises and 7% of Fortune 500 companies had female CEO in 2020.

Women's representation in parliament has more than doubled globally in the political sphere. But due to its meagre starting points, it has still not crossed the barrier of 25% parliamentary seats in 2020. Consequently, it will take over 200 years to reach gender equality in this area at the *current pace. Similarly, women's representation among cabinet minister has quadrupled over the last 25 years yet remains well below parity at 22%. Women's representation in the judiciary is generally better, but still not a the parity levels at the higher levels of judiciary posts.*

Improved education achievement, but issues remain

Marked progress has been made in achieving near-universal primary education, with girls and boys equal participation in most countries worldwide. Girls have also mostly caught up with boys regarding access to and graduation rates of secondary education. Data shows that girls tend to outperform boys in academic achievement once access to schooling is ensured. Furthermore, women outnumber men in tertiary education, with current trends pointing out the faster increase of enrolment rates for women compared to men.

However, there are numerous remaining concerns regarding gender equality in education. For example, women are severely underrepresented in the STEM fields, where they constitute only around 35% of STEM graduates globally. They are an even smaller minority in scientific research and development, representing less than a third of the world's researchers. Women are also far from parity in academic posts in universities and scientific institutions, with the proportion of women falling with each higher level of the academic hierarchy.

Persisting violence against women and girls

Women and girls continue to be victims of violence and physical abuse. Physical or sexual violence by an intimate partner has been experienced by around one-third of women worldwide. And around one-fifth of them have experienced such violence over the past 12 months. In the most extreme cases, such violence against women leads to lethal outcomes, with the global average of approximately 137 women killed by their intimate partner or a family member every day. For many women and girls, COVID-19 lockdowns have further complicated their situation. They have found themselves isolated in unsafe circumstances with a heightened risk of experiencing violence from intimate partners or household members. And although female genital mutilation rates are falling in some countries, there are currently at least 200 million women and girls who have suffered this form of violence.

Changes in attitudes are happening but are uneven and slow

Although generally difficult to change, attitudes, social norms, beliefs, and values, such changes are identified across societies and domains, including in the issues related to gender equality. It has been found that women's acceptance of being beaten by their partners decreased in almost 75% of countries over the past seven years. On the other hand, part of the reason for the slow pace of attitudinal change might be because the hurtful beliefs fuelling gender inequality are sometimes held by women almost as much as by men. For example, although it may be assumed that wife-beating is more widely justified by men, in the 53 countries with available attitudinal data, reported acceptance rates were lower among men than women in 40 of these countries.

Discriminatory attitudes lead to discriminatory behaviours, and these seem to be coming most often from those closest to women. Throughout the world, women face the highest levels of discrimination in their own households, especially regarding their responsibilities at home. Worldwide the level of discrimination in the family is 44%, compared to 29% in restrictive civil liberties, 28% in access to resources and 22% in restricted physical integrity.

Discriminatory attitudes toward women's participation in the labour market are persistent in most regions worldwide. Men were more likely to disapprove of women's employment outside of the home (20% versus 14%, respectively), and this disapproval was even higher with children present in the household. But even more alarmingly, women have expressed an almost equal preference with men for women to remain at home rather than work at a paid job or do both (27% versus 29%, respectively).

Legal frameworks are changing, but much work remains

An increasing number of countries are introducing gender parity principles in their legal frameworks. Fourteen additional countries introduced legislation to criminalise intimate partner violence, with 153 countries having such laws. Fifteen additional countries delayed the legal marriage age, and paid maternity leave is available in all but two countries.

On the other hand, 88 countries prescribe women from entering certain professions, and 24 countries require women to be permitted by their husbands to choose a profession or work. Moreover, 34 countries entitle husbands to solely administer and dispose of marital property, and 40 countries recognise the husband as head of household. Moreover, women don't have equal inheritance rights in 29 countries and cannot initiate divorce in 38 countries. And in whopping 119 countries around the world, women still face legal restrictions in the case of an unwanted pregnancy!

Available data must be interpreted with caution and awareness of their limitations

Data on which presented reports on the global status of gender equality vary vastly in their quality and relevance. As is the case in other areas of empirical research, what ends up being measured is not only determined by its importance but also by the ease of its measurability. This leads to the fact that some easily measurable aspects of gender equality are more prominent in available empirical analyses of this phenomenon. At the same time, some harder to measure aspects are often overlooked and absent from the empirical overviews and the sets of indicators on which global indices are constructed. For example, it is much easier to measure whether or not a woman has a job than whether or not a woman has a job in which she is treated equally and given the same rights and opportunities that she would have been given if she was men.

The lack of these harder-to-capture data means that the available empirical findings on gender equality, although offering valuable insights, should be interpreted with due care and caution. In other words, we should avoid seeing them (as they are sometimes intended to be seen) as the ultimate answers on the state of gender equality across the world and the reliable benchmarks of countries' global positions in this area. There are many gender equality issues that we are still straggling with grasping, let alone measuring with the required precision and validity. These shortcomings in our available evidence on gender equality should be considered when interpreting such data to avoid simplifying or misinterpreting the very reality that we are trying to change for the better.

Looking ahead – options and opportunities for action

Much work is needed to tackle existing gender inequalities in Australia and worldwide. In terms of the priorities for action, maybe the best principle would be to help the most those facing the most severe conditions. That would mean trying to first help women in some of the most populous and most in-need regions of the world, such as sub-Sahara, Middle-East, South Asia, and Central America. Regarding aspects of gender equality, the most pressing issue remains the high levels of physical and sexual violence against women and girls that persists in most of the world population. A related issue, and the one that is part of the root cause of many of the manifestations of gender inequality, are social norms and attitudes that are often inherently or explicitly discriminatory and harmful to women and girls. They are notoriously hard to change but investing in their change makes sense when one considers that such change would make all other aspects of gender equality much easier to tackle and improve efficiently, and vice versa. Finally, one of the most striking findings among the many presented in this report is that on the especially high levels of discrimination and violence women often face within the intimate confines of their own homes. Such a situation is at odds with the fact that most of the policy attention in this area is directed to the status of gender equality in various public spheres – work, education and health services, politics and citizenship. This is not to say that achieving equality in these areas is not important, but rather to point out that gender equality in public life is not possible nor meaningful if it is not based on equality in private life.

All in all, there are many possible targets of action, at local, national, regiona and global levels. But starting a policy action in the area of gender equality far from guarantees that such action will result in any observable improvements. In fact, the painfully slow pace of progress and apparent ineffectiveness of numerous national, regional and global gender equality initiatives indicates that these policy drives might be based on wrong premises or are overlooking important considerations. Such a situation indicates that any effort to improve things in this area must be more effective, relevant, tailor-made, comprehensive, and consistent. In other words, we not only need to do more than what we have been doing; we need to start doing it smarter. And for that to happen, we need to start getting a better understanding of which policy intervention works and which doesn't and the reasons behind such outcomes. These issues of the (lack of) effectiveness of policy interventions in gender equality will be the subject of the third scoping report on gender equality.

Abbreviations and acronyms

GDI Gender Development Index

GGGI The Global Gender Gap

GII Gender Inequality Index

HDI Human Development Index

LMICs Lower-middle-income countries

NGOs Non-governmental organisations

OECD Organisation for Economic Cooperation and Development

SDGs The Sustainable Development Goals

SIGI Social Institutions and Gender Index

STEM Science, technology, engineering, and mathematics

UN United Nations

UN DESA The United Nations Department of Economic and Social Affairs

UNDP United Nations Development Program

WEF World Economic Forum

WHO World Health Organization

Introduction

———

Despite the persistent data gaps, a large amount of empirical evidence on gender equality has been gathered worldwide, especially during the last few decades. This international data-gathering activity over the last decade largely revolved around the UN's 2030 Sustainable Development Goals (SDGs), but many other initiatives and empirical programs, both at the global, regional and national levels, have contributed as well. In this brief report, I will try to outline the key aspects of the available evidence on the state of gender equality worldwide. The report will start with an overview of the status of the SDGs in terms of gender equality, followed by a short outline of the main results across available global gender equality indices and other important global empirical programs. The report will also take a brief look into the regional results, and Australia's region in particular.

1. Gender Equality in the area of Sustainable Development Goals (SDGs)

Findings from the *Equal Measures 2030's* 2019 report on its SDG Index[1], designed to indicate the status of gender equality across 14 out of 17 SDGs in 129 countries, are presented in **Figure 1** (Equal Measures 2030, 2019). See **Appendices 1**, **2** and **3** for further finding on the fulfilment of gender-specific SDG indicators.

The 2019 SDG Gender Index finds that no country has fully achieved gender equality. It also shows a great deal of variation in the status of gender equality both across domains or SDG indicators and across countries and regions. The findings show that many countries from Europe and North America have achieved important milestones towards gender equality in several SDG domains, including education, health, access to essential services, legal frameworks, and so forth. Nevertheless, gathered data also indicates huge gaps among women and men in all world regions across many areas.

---

1. https://www.equalmeasures2030.org/wp-content/uploads/2021/06/ EM2030_2019_Global_Report_English_WEB-1.pdf

Figure 1: 2019 SDG Gender Index scores by goal, global averages

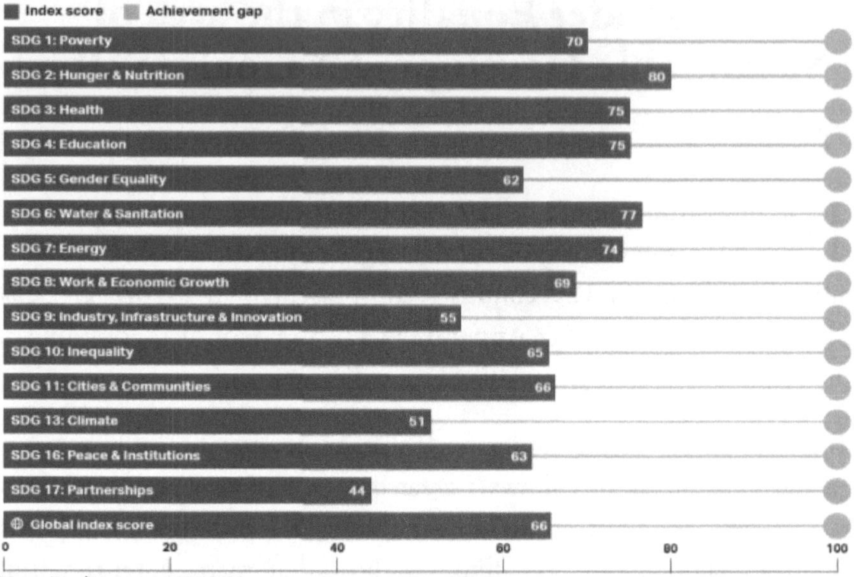

Source: Equal Measures 2030, 2019

Although many countries have achieved relatively high scores on this index, the overall picture at the country level generally tends to hide the severity of the gender gap across the world. That happens because the poorer countries and countries with lower levels of gender equality also tend to be more populous. This leads to a situation in which around 80% of the girls and women in the surveyed 129 countries live in countries that generally fail on gender equality or are in countries that "barely pass" (**Figure 2**)[1].

Figure 2: The number of girls and women living in countries by 2019 SDG Gender Index score grouping, in millions

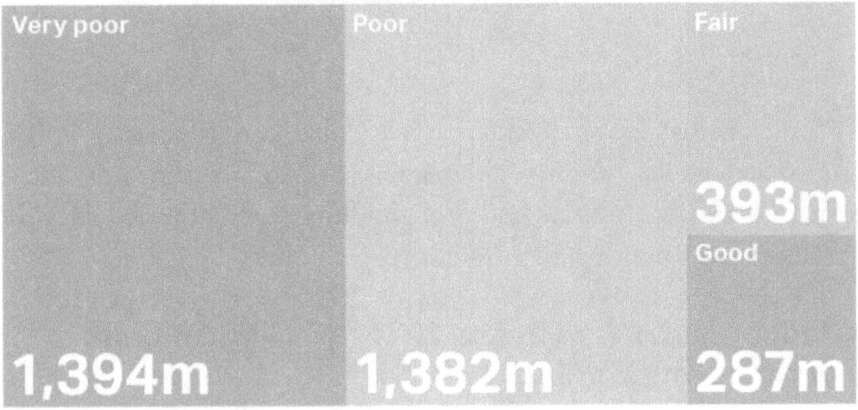

Source: Equal Measures 2030, (2019).

2. Global indices

Projects that have constructed few global gender equality indices show similar results, although their slightly different focus, structure, and data sources lead to slight differences in the country-level results on their indices and sub-indices.

Global Gender Gap Index, 2021 (World Economic Forum) – Key Findings

The World Economic Forum's Global Gender Gap Index[1] tracks the evolution of gender-based gaps and tracks progress towards closing these gaps over time. In its 2021 round[2], the Global Gender Gap Index gathered data from 156 countries, providing a comprehensive tool for global comparisons and benchmarking (WEF, 2021). The Global Gender Gap Index construct scores on a 0 to 100 scale, representing the distance to gender parity (i.e., the percentage of the gender gap that is closed).

Similar to the SDG Index discussed previously, the GGG Index indicates that women, on average globally and across various domains, have only around two-thirds of the rights and resources available to men. However, such an average hides quite a different picture across domains. For example, globally, women are relatively close to gender parity in education and health domains. On the other hand, the gender gap is much larger in terms of their economic participation. The worst situation is in the domain of political participation, where women enjoy less than a quarter of the rights and resources compared to men (**Figure 3**).

---

1. https://www.weforum.org/reports/ab6795a1-960c-42b2-b3d5-587eccda6023

2. https://www3.weforum.org/docs/WEF_GGGR_2021.pdf

Figure 3: The state of gender gaps, by sub-index

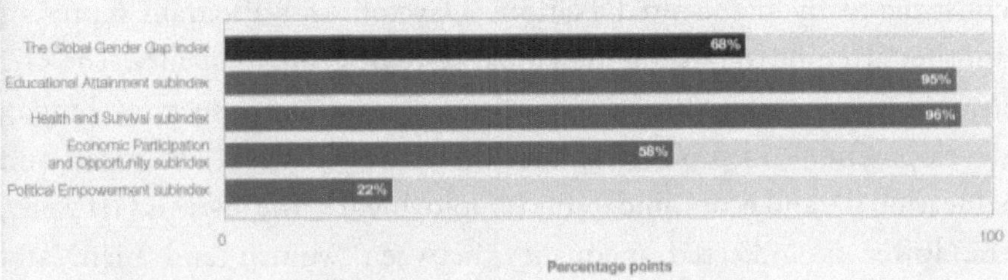

Source: World Economic Forum, Global Gender Gap Index, 2021.

Here again, the gender (in)equality differs markedly across countries and regions, with some countries, like Chad, failing to achieve educational parity while others, like Iceland, largely closing the gap even in terms of political participation and empowerment (**Figure 4**).

Figure 4: Variation of country scores across the Global Gender Gap Index and sub-indices, 2021

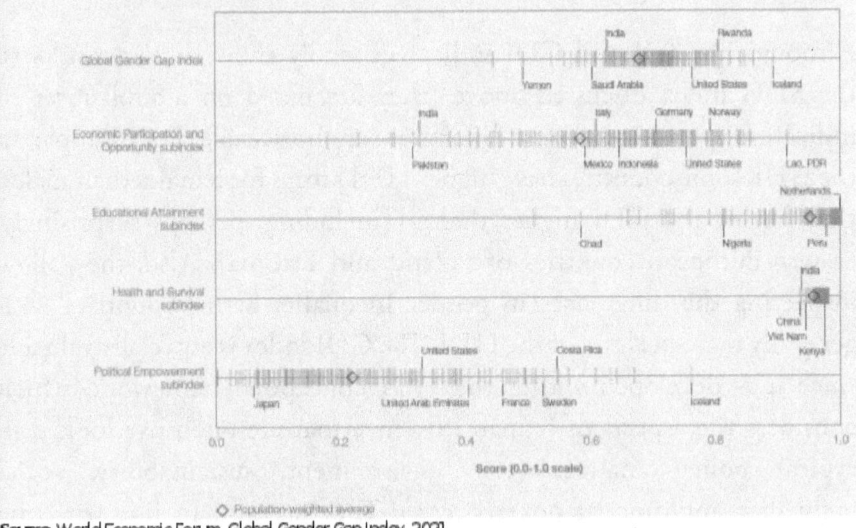

Source: World Economic Forum, Global Gender Gap Index, 2021.

Gender Inequality Index (GII) and Gender

Development Index (GDP) - UNDP

The Gender Inequality Index and Gender Development Index constructed by the United Nations Development Program represent another attempt to outline the global state of gender equality. The GII assesses gender inequalities across three important aspects of human development – reproductive health, empowerment (political and educational), and economic status (employment). The lower is GII value, the lower is indicated inequality between women and men, and vice-versa.

The Gender Development Index (GDI) measures disparities in the UNDP flagship Human Development Index (HDI) by gender. In particular, the HDI values are estimated separately for women and men, the ratio of which is the GDI value. The ratio that is closer to 1 indicates a smaller gender gap. In addition, values for the three HDI components — longevity, education (with two indicators), and income per capita — are also presented by gender.

Although the GII and GDI indices generally show similar results to the SDG index discussed above (they are based on a similar set of indicators), some important differences are noticeable. For example, in the GDI, some countries have higher HDI scores for females than males, thus having the GDI higher than 1 (including, perhaps surprisingly, eastern-European countries of Poland and Estonia). Also, they allow inspecting the differences in gender inequality across countries with generally the same level of the HDI. The GDI index is especially valuable since it is developed within the HDI conceptual framework, which considers the aspects of human existence that are often overlooked in typical policy analyses (e.g., environment, sustainability, social inequality, multimodal poverty, etc.). They are also in line with the empirical observations of human mortality (a very high correlation between the HDI and mortality at the country level), indicating that they are capturing something crucial. Furthermore, being done by the UN organisation, they include data from basically all countries and territories in the world, thus having vastly broader populational coverage than the WEF's GGG Index.

The Social Institutions and Gender Index (SIGI) – Key Findings

The Social Institutions and Gender Index (SIGI) is an especially important empirical project. It aims to measure the invisible part of gender equality by examining the gaps that discriminatory legislation, attitudes, social norms, and practices create between women and men regarding their rights and opportunities. The SIGI index combines data from 33 indicators on the level of discrimination in laws, social norms, and practices. It draws comprehensive information on legal frameworks and action plans to protect women's rights in 180 countries and classifies 120 countries according to the level of discrimination embedded in their social institutions. By combining the analysis of the legal and policy environment with data on people's gender attitudes, it reflects both the *de jure* state of laws and the *de facto* situation on the ground. Importantly, by collecting data during several rounds over the last decade, the SIGI index can also show trends across its four dimensions: discrimination in the family, restricted access to productive and financial resources, restricted physical integrity, and restricted civil liberties.

The key findings of the SIGI 2019 report[3] are that progress has been made towards greater gender equality, most notably in the legal frameworks (OECD, 2019). New legislation that enhances equality and abolishes discriminatory laws has been enacted. In the last five years, 14 countries have criminalised domestic violence, and 15 countries have strengthened their legal frameworks to delay the age of first marriage by eliminating legal exceptions allowing girls to be married. Additionally,

---

3. https://www.oecd.org/development/sigi-2019-global-report-bc56d212-en.htm

gender-sensitive programs have positively affected certain discriminatory social norms, making them less prominent. As a result, social acceptance of domestic violence has decreased from 50% in 2012 to 27% in 2018.

However, despite the progress made, it will take over 200 years, or nine generations, to achieve gender equality at the current pace. Political commitments, legal reforms and gender-sensitive programs in many countries are still not translated into real change. As a result, the number of girl marriages and women's labour participation has stagnated, and slow progress has been made in the prevalence of domestic violence and women's political participation. The report indicates that slow progress is due to existing legal discrimination and loopholes, the inadequacy of existing laws and programs, the uneven implementation and enforcement of the law within and across countries, and the persistence of discriminatory customary laws and social norms.

Throughout the world, women face the highest levels of discrimination in their own households, especially regarding their responsibilities at home. Worldwide the level of discrimination in the family is 44%, compared to 29% in restrictive civil liberties, 28% in access to resources and 22% in restricted physical integrity. In some countries, laws and social norms governing family matters still consider a woman as a dependent household member subordinate to her husband's authority. For instance, 40 countries still solely recognise the husband as the head of the household, and 27 countries require women to obey their husbands. Even in Europe and the Americas, women's roles are confined to their traditional reproductive and caring responsibilities, spending 2 and 3 times more time in unpaid care and domestic work. Further details of the key findings of the SIGI 2019 report are given in **Appendix 4**.

3. Other global results

———

As noted in the first landscape report, many other relevant and informative data sources on gender equality bring upon new information and show additional aspects of the global state of gender equality. However, a detailed review of these would fall out of the scope of this brief report. I will here shortly outline only a few of these programs.

UN Women's reports are one of the most informative and authoritative sources of empirical data on the status of gender equality around the world. Since they are collecting information from other UN agencies on gender equality, they offer some of the most comprehensive empirical overviews of the topic. They are also producing a vast set of publications in a reader-friendly and visually appealing way. I will present their findings in two less explored areas: legal equality and equality in family decision-making (**Figure 5** and **Figure 6**).

Figure 5: Proportion of countries with or without legal equality in selected areas of law, 2018

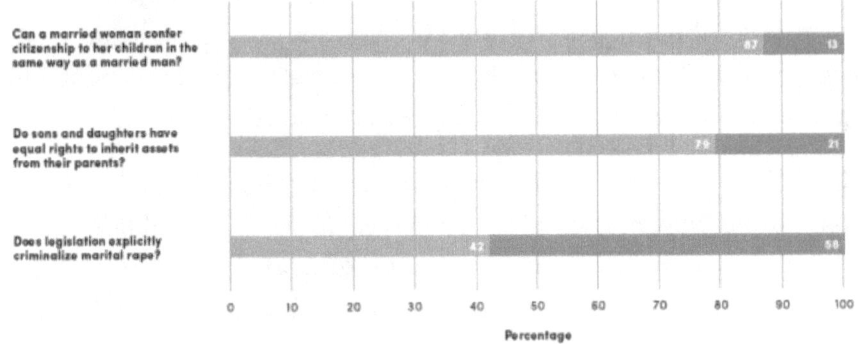

Source: UN Women (2019) calculations based on the World Bank (2018) data

Figure 6: Decision-making by age at the first union, currently married/in union, women aged 19-49

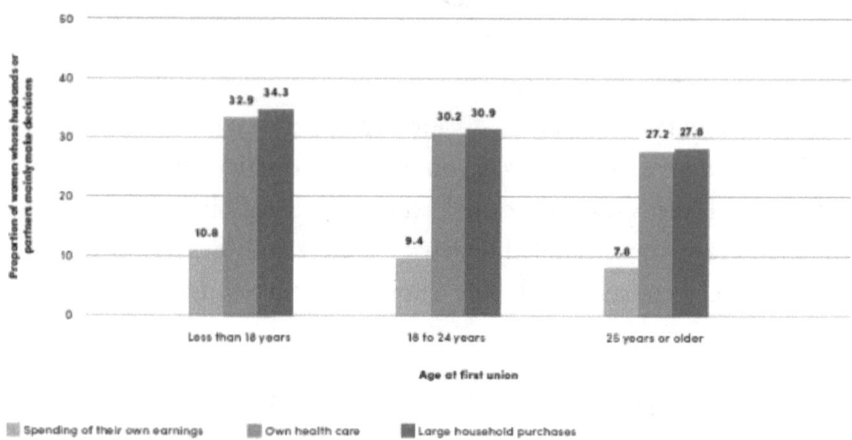

Source: UN Women (2019) calculations based on ICF International 2007-2017, Demographic and Health Surveys

The World Bank's research and empirical data repository provide some of the most comprehensive information on key aspects of gender equality across the world. Its findings on the status of gender equality globally and in Australia in particular, from one of its flagship publications, are available in **Appendices 8** and **9**. Its special value is that it allows for a comparison of the data across two decades, observing the changes or lack of them across various indicators. So, we can see, for example, that political participation (indicated by seats held in parliaments) has significantly increased over this period, but also that the labour force participation rate of women has decreased over this period.

OECD is another important player in the field of gathering and publishing empirical data on gender equality. Their publications on *'Gender Equality in Politics'* (OECD, 2021a), *'Gender Equality in Judiciary'* (OECD, 2021b) and *'Gender Equality in Public Sector Employment'* (OECD, 2021c) are particularly noteworthy. Here we present their findings on 'gender budgeting', a practice that helps ensure that considerations for gender equality are systematically incorporated into budget decisions (**Figure 7**).

Figure 7: Composite indicator on gender budgeting in OECD countries, 2018

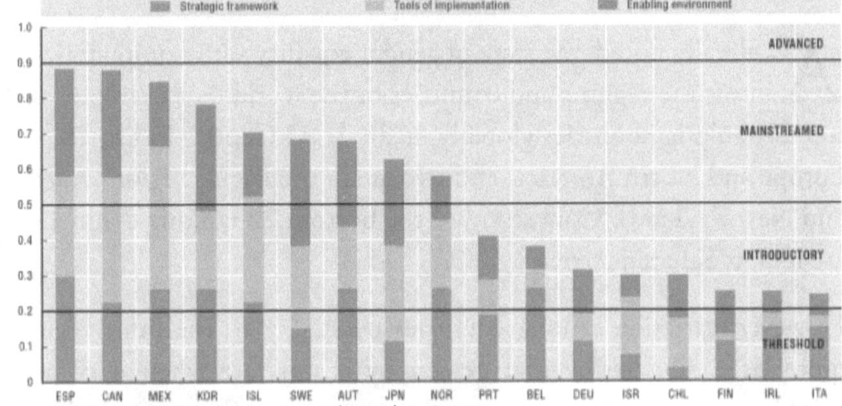

Source: OECD (2018), OECD Budget Practices and Procedures Survey.

4. Regional results

As already noted, the state of gender equality varies quite drastically across the regions and countries of the world. For example, of the top 20 ranking countries globally in the SDG Gender Index, 18 are in Europe and North America, and two are in the Pacific region (Australia and New Zealand). Conversely, of the bottom 20 ranking countries, 17 are in Sub-Saharan Africa.

However, variation among countries belonging to the same region is quite large, illustrating that geography is not fate when it comes to gender equality. For example, every region has a difference of at least 17 points in SDG Gender Index scores between a top and bottom ranking country. Even in Latin America and the Caribbean, which has the least variation of any region, countries are spread across "very poor", "poor", and "fair" scores (**Figure 8**).

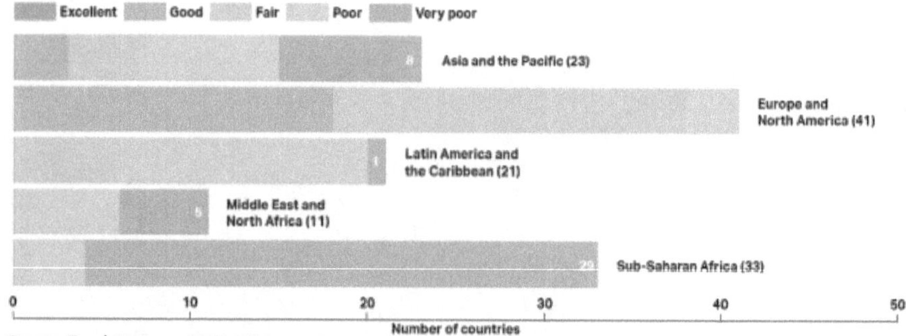

Figure 8: Number of countries by 2019 SDG Gender Index score grouping

Source: Equal Measures 2030, 2019

Large regional gaps are evident in other global overviews and indices, including the WEF's Global Gender Gap Index (**Figure 9**).

Figure 9: Regional scores on the Global Gender Gap Index, World Economic Forum, 2021

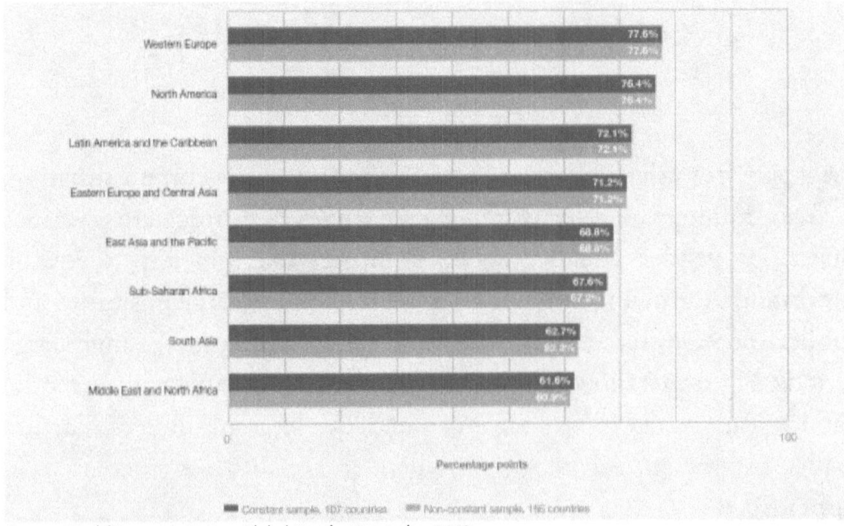

Source: World Economic Forum, Global Gender Gap Index, 2021

5. Global trends/changes in gender equality in recent decades

Apart from the cross-sectional descriptions of the current situation, examining the general trends or changes occurring across various aspects of gender equality across countries and globally is equally important. A growing number of presented empirical depositories and publications are starting to track these trends across increasingly large periods. **Figure 10** shows the Global Gender Gap Index changes over the last 15 years across its overall index and the four sub-indices. Further results on the global changes in gender equality are presented in **Appendix 6**.

Figure 10: Evolution of the Global Gender Gap Index and sub-indices over time (2006-2021)

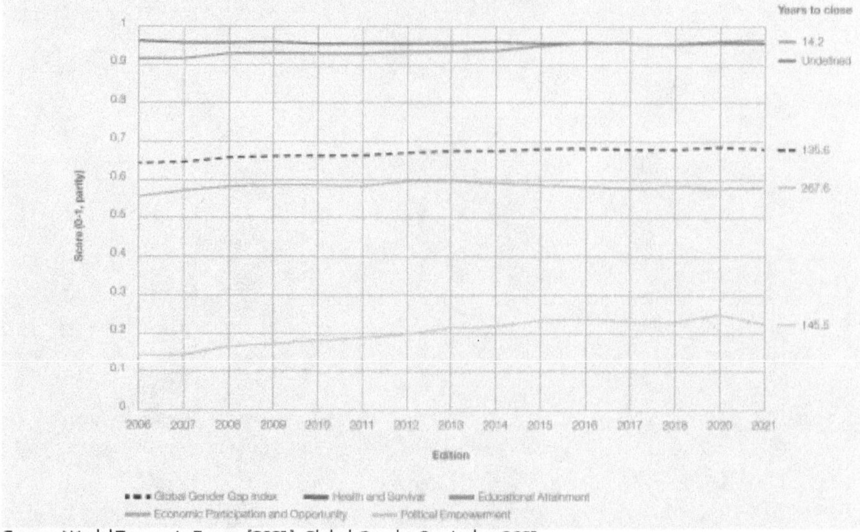

Source: World Economic Forum (2021), Global Gender Gap Index, 2021.

These findings indicate that, in general, there is rather slow progress on various aspects of gender equality around the world. Importantly, the pace of progress somewhat differs across domains of gender equality, with relatively faster improvements occurring in political empowerment and much less so in the area of economic participation. Regretfully, the direction of change is not always towards greater gender equality, with growing inequality appearing in some domains and some regions. For example, the World Bank's data in **Appendix 8** show that women's labour market participation dropped from 51% in 2000 to 48% in 2017 (World Bank, 2019). Likewise, World Economic Forum's data indicate a substantial drop in political empowerment in South Asia over the last year (World Economic Forum, 2021; see **Appendix 6**). In addition, OECD has found that the proportion of women in parliaments has dropped in the number of OECD countries (**Appendix 6**).

Nevertheless, there is still marked progress in some areas and some regions. For example, the completion rate of primary school for girls has increased from 79% in 2000 to 90% in 2017, basically closing the gender gap in this indicator. And the tertiary enrolment ratio (% of relevant age group) has jumped from 19% in 2000 to 40% in 2017, which is larger than the same proportion for males (36%). Likewise, the region of Latin America has experienced especially noticeable progress across a range of gender equality aspects, resulting in an increase of its Global Gender Gap index from .64 in 2006 to .73 in 2021. It should also be noted that women are better off than men in some researched aspects (e.g., longevity, sickness, tertiary graduation rates, academic achievement). That might be the reason why the UNDP's Gender Development Index indicates that the status of human development (as measured in their Human Development Index) in some countries is slightly higher for women than for men. However, although these findings should be considered, they also reflect some of the methodological and substantive shortcomings of the available empirical evidence these global indices are based on.

6. Summary

The world is still a long way from gender equality. Over and over again, women are given fewer opportunities or are treated worse than men in comparable situations. This inequality spreads across different aspects of women's everyday lives, although it varies across these domains in terms of its severity and characteristics. Moreover, gender equality is markedly different across countries and regions worldwide. For example, of the top 20 ranking countries globally in the UN's SDG Gender Index, 18 are in Europe and North America, and two are in the Pacific region (Australia and New Zealand). Conversely, of the bottom 20 ranking countries, 17 are in Sub-Saharan Africa. So, while some northern-European countries are reaching or even exceeding parity levels across many areas, women in several world regions face incredibly high levels of inequality and even violence and abuse.

Furthermore, although many developed countries achieve relatively high scores on various global gender equality indices, the overall picture at the country level generally tends to hide the severity of the gender gap across the world. That happens because the poorer countries and countries with lower levels of gender equality also tend to be more populous. That leads to a situation where around 80% of the girls and women in the participating sample of 129 countries live in countries that generally "fail" or "barely pass" on gender equality.

Available trend data identify various changes in the levels of gender equality around the world, although their magnitude and direction are not always as expected or desired. On the positive side, the empirical evidence shows that things are changing for the better in several areas of gender equality at the global level. These include markedly better education outcomes for girls and higher levels of political participation.

Nevertheless, the progress has generally been painfully slow, and it has occasionally taken a turn for the worse in some areas and regions.

Lack of progress in the area of economic empowerment

Women continue to do most of the unpaid domestic care and work, although this kind of work has intensified for both men and women during the COVID-19 pandemic. Currently, on an average day globally, women spend about two and a half times more doing unpaid care and domestic work than men (4.2 hours compared to 1.7, respectively). What is more, this uneven distribution of unpaid domestic and care work prevents women from participating in the labour market.

As a result, less than 50% of working-age women are in the labour market, a figure that is lower today than twenty years ago (World Bank, 2021; **Appendix 5**). In comparison with 74% of employed men, the employment gap is huge and persistent. Moreover, the pandemic is expected to exacerbate these gender disparities. Many women work in the sectors hardest hit by COVID-19 measures, including paid domestic work, hospitality and catering services, and the retail industry.

Few cracks in the glass ceiling

In areas of political and economic power and decision-making, the situation is changing for the better, while in others, it is largely stagnating. But in all of the available indicators, the gap between women and men regarding power access and the ability to participate in decision-making is vast. Women were still holding only 28% of managerial positions globally in 2019, almost the same percentage as in 1995. Only 18% of enterprises and 7% of Fortune 500 companies had female CEO in 2020.

Women's representation in parliament has more than doubled globally in the political sphere. But due to its meagre starting points, it has still not crossed the barrier of 25% parliamentary seats in 2020. Consequently, it will take over 200 years to reach gender equality in this area at the current pace. Similarly, women's representation among cabinet ministers has quadrupled over the last 25 years yet remains well below parity at 22%. Women's representation in the judiciary is generally better, but still not at the parity levels at the higher levels of judiciary posts.

Improved education achievement, but issues remain

Marked progress has been made in achieving near-universal primary education, with girls and boys equal participation in most countries worldwide. Girls have also mostly caught up with boys regarding access to and graduation rates of secondary education. Data shows that girls tend to outperform boys in academic achievement once access to schooling is ensured. Furthermore, women outnumber men in tertiary education, with current trends pointing out the faster increase of enrolment rates for women compared to men.

However, there are numerous remaining concerns regarding gender equality in education. For example, women are severely underrepresented in the STEM fields, where they constitute only around 35% of STEM graduates globally. They are an even smaller minority in scientific research and development, representing less than a third of the world's researchers. Women are also far from parity in academic posts in universities and scientific institutions, with the proportion of women falling with each higher level of the academic hierarchy.

Persisting violence against women and girls

Women and girls continue to be victims of violence and physical abuse. Physical or sexual violence by an intimate partner has been experienced by around one-third of women worldwide. And around one-fifth of them have experienced such violence over the past 12 months. In the most extreme cases, such violence against women leads to lethal outcomes, with the global average of approximately 137 women killed by their intimate partner or a family member every day. For many women and girls, COVID-19 lockdowns have further complicated their situation, as they have found themselves isolated in unsafe circumstances with a heightened risk of experiencing violence from intimate partners or household members. And although female genital mutilation rates are falling in some countries, there are currently at least 200 million women and girls who have suffered this form of violence.

Changes in attitudes are happening but are uneven and slow

Although generally difficult to change, attitudes, social norms, beliefs, and values, such changes are identified across societies and domains, including in the issues related to gender equality. It has been found that women's acceptance of being beaten by their partners decreased in almost 75% of countries over the past seven years. On the other hand, part of the reason for the slow pace of attitudinal change might be because the hurtful beliefs fuelling gender inequality are sometimes held by women almost as much as by men. For example, although it may be assumed that wife-beating is more widely justified by men, in the 53 countries with available attitudinal data, reported acceptance rates were lower among men than women in 40 of these countries.

Discriminatory attitudes lead to discriminatory behaviours, and these seem to be coming most often from those closest to women. Throughout the world, women face the highest levels of discrimination in their own households, especially regarding their responsibilities at home. Worldwide the level of discrimination in the family is 44%, compared to 29% in restrictive civil liberties, 28% in access to resources and 22% in restricted physical integrity.

Discriminatory attitudes toward women's participation in the labour market are persistent in most regions worldwide. Men were more likely to disapprove of women's employment outside of the home (20% versus 14%, respectively), and this disapproval was even higher with children present in the household. But even more alarmingly, women have expressed an almost equal preference with men for women to remain at home rather than work at a paid job or do both (27% versus 29%, respectively).

Legal frameworks are changing, but much work remains

An increasing number of countries are introducing gender parity principles in their legal frameworks. Fourteen additional countries introduced legislation to criminalise intimate partner violence, with 153 countries having such laws. Fifteen additional countries delayed the legal marriage age, and paid maternity leave is available in all but two countries.

On the other hand, 88 countries prescribe women from entering certain professions, and 24 countries require women to be permitted by their husbands to choose a profession or work. Moreover, 34 countries entitle husbands to administer and dispose of marital property solely, and 40 countries recognise the husband as head of household. Moreover, women don't have equal inheritance rights in 29 countries and cannot initiate divorce in 38 countries. And in whopping 119 countries around the world, women still face legal restrictions in the case of an unwanted pregnancy!

Available data must be interpreted with caution and awareness of their limitations

Data on which presented reports on the global status of gender equality vary vastly in their quality and relevance. As is the case in other areas of empirical research, what ends up being measured is not only determined by its importance but also by the ease of its measurability. This leads to the fact that some easily measurable aspects of gender equality are more prominent in available empirical analyses of this phenomenon. At the same time, some harder to measure aspects are often overlooked and absent from the empirical overviews and the sets of indicators on which global indices are constructed. For example, it is much easier to measure whether or not a woman has a job than whether or not a woman has a job in which she is treated equally and given the same rights and opportunities that she would have been given if she was men.

The lack of these harder-to-capture data means that the available empirical findings on gender equality, although offering valuable insights, should be interpreted with due care and caution. In other words, we should avoid seeing them (as they are sometimes intended to be seen) as the ultimate answers on the state of gender equality across the world and the reliable benchmarks of countries' global positions in this area. There are many gender equality issues that we are still straggling with grasping, let alone measuring with the required precision and validity. These shortcomings in our available evidence on gender equality should be considered when interpreting such data to avoid simplifying or misinterpreting the very reality that we are trying to change for the better.

Looking ahead – options and opportunities for action

Much work is needed to tackle existing gender inequalities in Australia and across the world. In terms of the priorities for action, maybe the best principle would be to help the most those facing the most severe conditions. That would mean trying to first help women in some of the most populous and most in-need regions of the world, such as sub-Sahara, Middle-East, South Asia, and Central America. Regarding aspects of gender equality, the most pressing issue remains high levels of physical and sexual violence against women and girls that persists in most of the world population. A related issue, and the one that is part of the root cause of many of the manifestations of gender inequality, are social norms and attitudes that are often inherently or explicitly discriminatory and harmful to women and girls. They are notoriously hard to change but investing in their change makes sense when one considers that such change would make all other aspects of gender equality much easier to tackle and improve efficiently, and vice versa. Finally, one of the most striking findings among the many presented in this report is that on the especially high levels of discrimination and violence women often face within the intimate confines of their own homes. Such a situation is at odds with the fact that most of the policy attention in this area is directed to the status of gender equality in various public spheres – work, education and health services, politics and citizenship. This is not to say that achieving equality in these areas is not important, but rather to point out that gender equality in public life is not possible nor meaningful if it is not based on equality in private life.

All in all, there are many possible targets of action, at local, national, regiona and global levels. But starting a policy action in the area of gender equality far from guarantees that such action will result in any observable improvements. In fact, the painfully slow pace of progress and apparent ineffectiveness of numerous national, regional and global gender equality initiatives indicates that these policy drives might be based on wrong premises or are overlooking important considerations. Such a situation indicates that any effort to improve things in this area must be more effective, relevant, tailor-made, comprehensive, and consistent. In other words, we not only need to do more than what we have been doing; we need to start doing it smarter. And for that to happen, we need to start getting a better understanding of which policy intervention works and which doesn't and the reasons behind such outcomes. These issues of the (lack of) effectiveness of policy interventions in gender equality will be the subject of the third scoping report on gender equality.

References

Equal Measures 2030 (2019). Harnessing The Power Of Data for Gender Equality: Introducing the 2019 EM2030 SDG Gender Index. https://www.equalmeasures2030.org/wp-content/uploads/2021/06/EM2030_2019_Global_Report_English_WEB-1.pdf

ITU (International Telecomunication Union), (2017), ICT Facts and Figures 2017. Geneva: ITU.

OECD (2012), *Closing the Gender Gap: Act Now*, OECD Publishing, Paris, http://dx.doi.org/10.1787/9789264179370-en.

OECD (2018). Budget Practices and Procedures Survey.

OECD (2019), SIGI 2019 Global Report: Transforming Challenges into Opportunities, Social Institutions and Gender Index, OECD Publishing, Paris, https://doi.org/10.1787/bc56d212-en.

OECD (2021a). Gender equality in politics, https://doi.org/10.1787/b4beed4b-en.

OECD (2021b). Gender equality in judiciary, https://doi.org/10.1787/2f520410-en.

OECD (2021c). Gender equality in public sector employment, https://doi.org/10.1787/7f55c675-en.

Open Data Watch and UNESCAP (2019). Bridging the Gap: Mapping Gender Data Availability in Asia and the Pacific, https://data2x.org/wp-content/uploads/ 2019/06/ Bridging-the-Gap- Technical-Report-Web-Ready.pdf

UN Women (2018). Turning promises into action: Gender equality in the 2030 Agenda for Sustainable Development https://www.unwomen.org/en/digital- library/publications/ 2018/2/gender-   equality-in-the-2030-agenda-for-sustainable-development-2018

UN Women (2019). Progress of the World's Women 2019-2020: Families in a Changing World. https://doi.org/ 10.18356/696a9392-en

UN (2017). The Sustainable Development Goals Report 2017. New York: United Nations.

UN (2019). Progress towards the Sustainable Development Goals : report of the Secretary-General, https://digitallibrary.un.org/record/ 3810131?ln=en

UN DESA (United Nations Department of Economic and Social Affairs) (2020). The World's Women 2020: Trends and Statistics,   https://worlds-women-2020-data-undesa.hub.arcgis.com.

UNDP (2020). Human Development Report: The next frontier Human development and the Anthropocene.

World Economic Forum (2021). Global Gender Gap Report 2021,   https://www3.weforum.org/docs/WEF_GGGR_2021.pdf

World Bank (2018). Women, Business and the Law. https://wbl.worldbank.org/#.

World Bank (2019). The Little Data Book on Gender 2019. World Bank, Washington, DC. © World Bank. https://openknowledg e.worldbank.org/ handle/10986/ 31689

Appendices

Appendix 1: Overview of the progress on the fulfilment of the SDGs across gender-specific indicators

UN Women – Sustainable Development Goals – Global Fact Sheet of Progress[2]

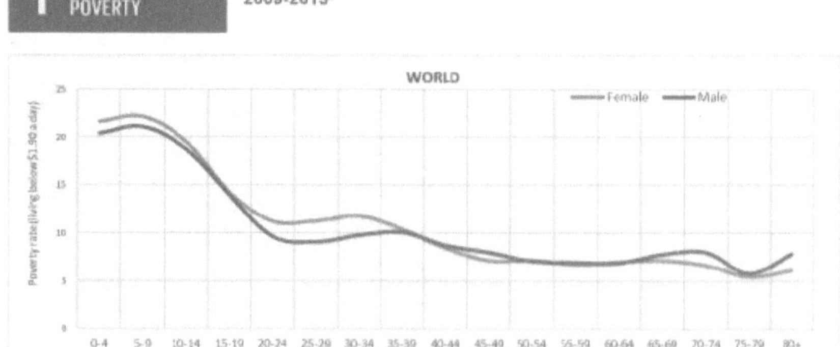

Source: World Bank calculations using Global Micro Database 2017.

2 ZERO HUNGER — Gender gap in prevalence of food security, 2014-2015

SDG Regional Groupings	% of females who are food insecure	% of males who are food insecure	Difference (f-m)
Australia and New Zealand	8.2	10.9	-2.7
Eastern Asia and South-eastern Asia	8.4	8.7	-0.3
Sub-Saharan Africa	56.7	56.1	0.6
Europe and Northern America	9.0	8.0	1.0
Northern Africa and Western Asia	28.8	26.8	2
Latin America and the Caribbean	30.8	28.0	2.8
Central Asia and Southern Asia	28.2	24.5	3.7
World	23.9	22.4	1.5

Souce: UN Women calculations based on data from the FAO Food Insecurity Experience Scale (FIES) survey (2014-2015).

5 GENDER EQUALITY — Internet penetration rate by sex and region, 2017

SDG Regional Groupings	Female Internet users as % of total female population 2017	Male Internet users as % of total male population 2017
Australia and New Zealand	53.7	56.9
Central and Southern Asia	41.5	44.6
Eastern and South-eastern Asia	27.8	42.0
Europe and Northern America	75.2	82.0
Latin America and the Caribbean	66.7	65.2
Northern Africa and Western Asia	55.3	59.5
Oceania (excluding Australia and New Zealand)	53.7	56.7
Sub-Saharan Africa	18.4	24.6
World	44.7	50.6

Source: ITU (International Telecomunication Union), (2017), ICT Facts and Figures 2017. Geneva: ITU.

11 SUSTAINABLE CITIES AND COMMUNITIES — Proportion of urban population living in slums (per cent)

Region	2014	2000
Australia and New Zealand	0.03	0.03
Central Asia and Southern Asia	31.89	46.05
Eastern Asia and South-Eastern Asia	27.55	38.23
Landlocked Developing Countries	59.00	67.11
Latin America and the Caribbean	21.26	29.31
Least developed countries	62.16	77.97
Northern America and Europe	0.10	0.10
Oceania (excluding Australia and New Zealand)	24.15	24.19
Sub-Saharan Africa	55.99	65.04
Western Asia and Northern Africa	22.06	23.11
World	22.77	28.42

Source: UN-Habitat, 2017.

The Sustainable Development Goals Report – 2020 (United Nations)

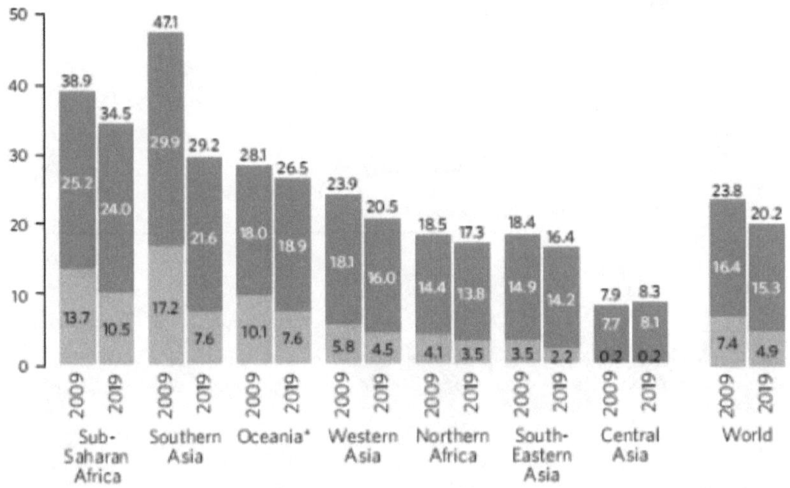

Source: UN (2017). The Sustainable Development Goals Report 2017.

Proportion of time spent on unpaid domestic and care work, women and men, 2001–2018 (latest available) (percentage of time spent per day)

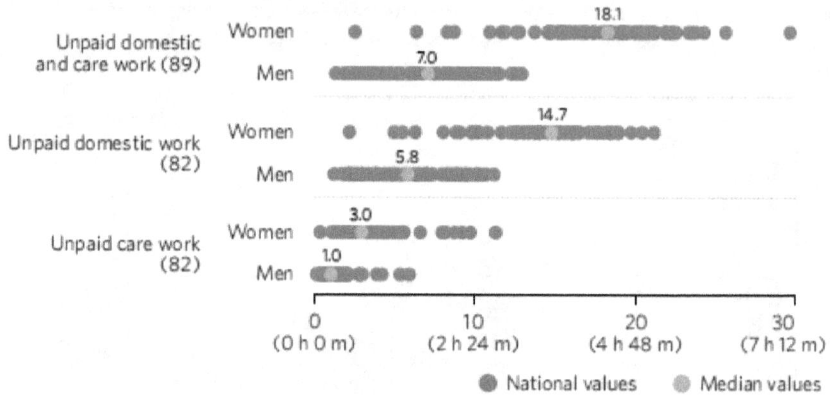

Note: The figure reflects available data for 89 countries and areas over the period 2001–2018. The number of countries and areas represented in each type of unpaid work is indicated in parentheses.

Source: UN (2017). The Sustainable Development Goals Report 2017.

Proportion of women aged 15 to 49 years who make their own decisions regarding sexual and reproductive health and rights, most recent data 2007–2018 (percentage)

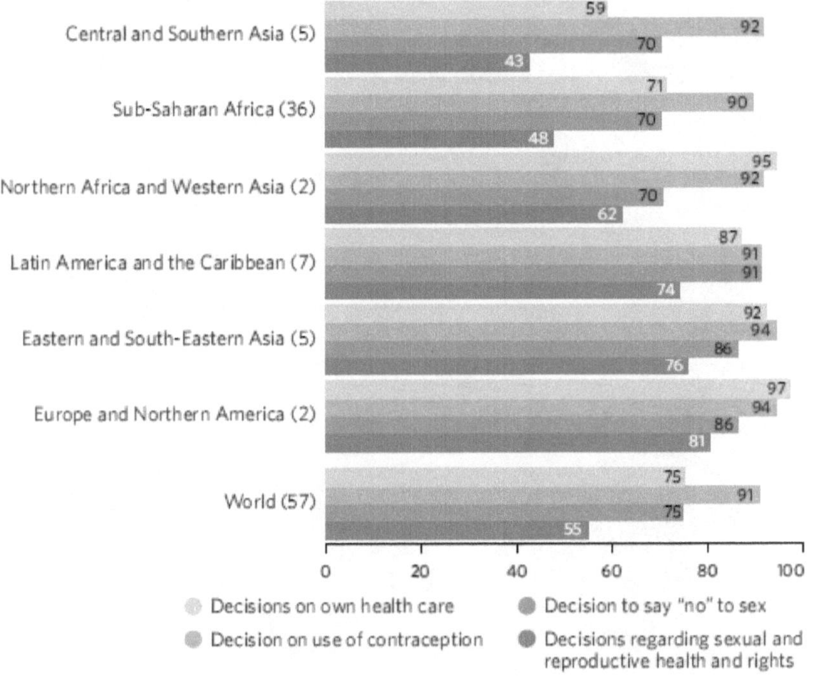

Note: The number of countries with comparable survey data included in the regional aggregations is presented in parentheses.

Source: UN (2017). The Sustainable Development Goals Report 2017.

Appendix 2; The World's Women: Trends and Statistics[3]

COVID-19 IS AFFECTING WOMEN AND MEN DIFFERENTLY

Women above age 20 appear to be more likely to be diagnosed with COVID-19, while men in all age groups under age 80 are more likely to die from it.

WOMEN ARE ON THE FRONT LINES OF FIGHTING THE CORONAVIRUS

THE "GLASS CEILING" STILL KEEPS WOMEN OUT OF STRATEGIC FUNCTIONS

The "glass ceiling" still keeps women in support management positions rather than allowing them access to strategic management functions.

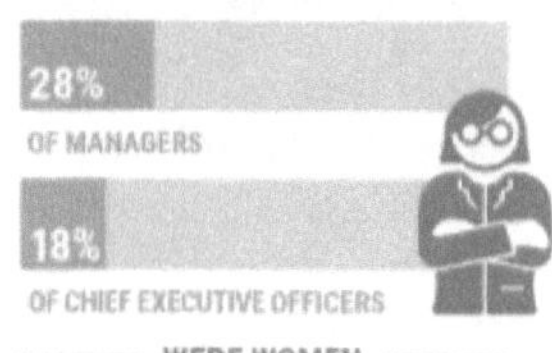

WOMEN REPRESENT

DOUBLE BURDEN FOR WOMEN: CARE GIVERS AND GREATER RISK OF ALZHEIMER'S

Marked gender differences in health and mortality patterns are also present in older ages. Women face a double burden: not only they are at higher risk of dementia as they live into older ages, they are also likely to be the main caregivers as partners, daughters and daughters-in-law.

LONGEVITY HAS IMPLICATIONS IN WOMEN'S LIVES, HEALTH AND WELL-BEING

Gender disparities in longevity in favour of women have implications in their living arrangements as well as for their health and well-being.

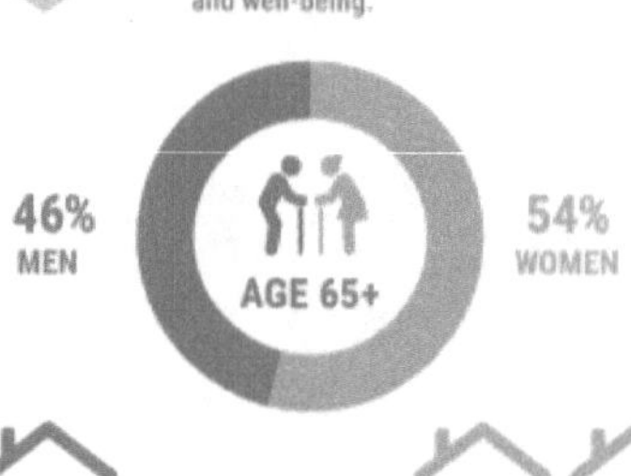

GENDER DISPARITIES PERSIST IN THE FIELDS OF STUDY AND WORK

In tertiary education, enrolment is increasing faster for women than for men. However, gender disparities persist in the fields of study chosen by women and men. Women continue to be underrepresented among graduates in the STEM fields and in ICT jobs.

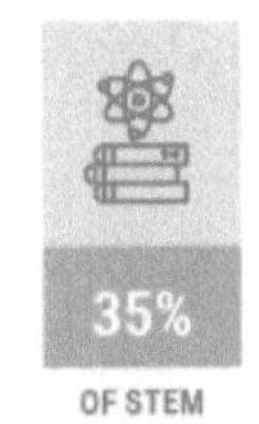

HEAVIER LOADS OF UNPAID WORK KEEP WOMEN OUT OF THE LABOUR MARKET

Family responsibilities and the unequal distribution of unpaid domestic and care work between women and men add to women's daily work and may prevent them from participating in the labour market.

SPENT BY WOMEN
ON UNPAID DOMESTIC AND CARE WORK
MORE THAN MEN

INTIMATE PARTNER VIOLENCE IS THE MOST COMMON FORM OF VIOLENCE AGAINST WOMEN

Intimate partner violence is the most common form of violence, peaking during women's reproductive years in both developed and developing countries.

Appendix 3: SDG Index (Equal Measures 2030 initiative)

2019 SDG Index scores and national per capita income (Equal Measures 2030 & World Bank)

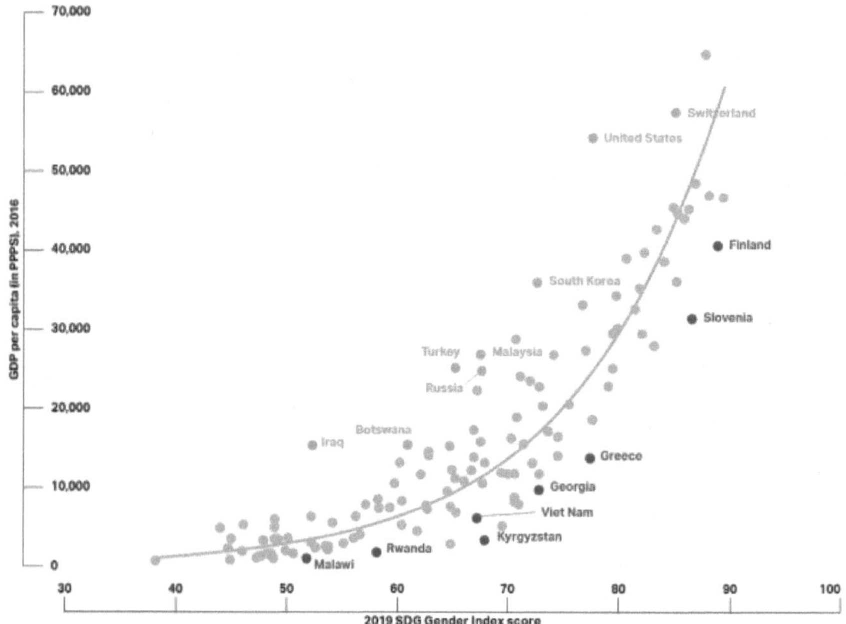

Sources: Equal Measures 2030, (2019) and World Bank, (2018).

Appendix 4: Social Institutions and Gender Index (SIGI), 2019

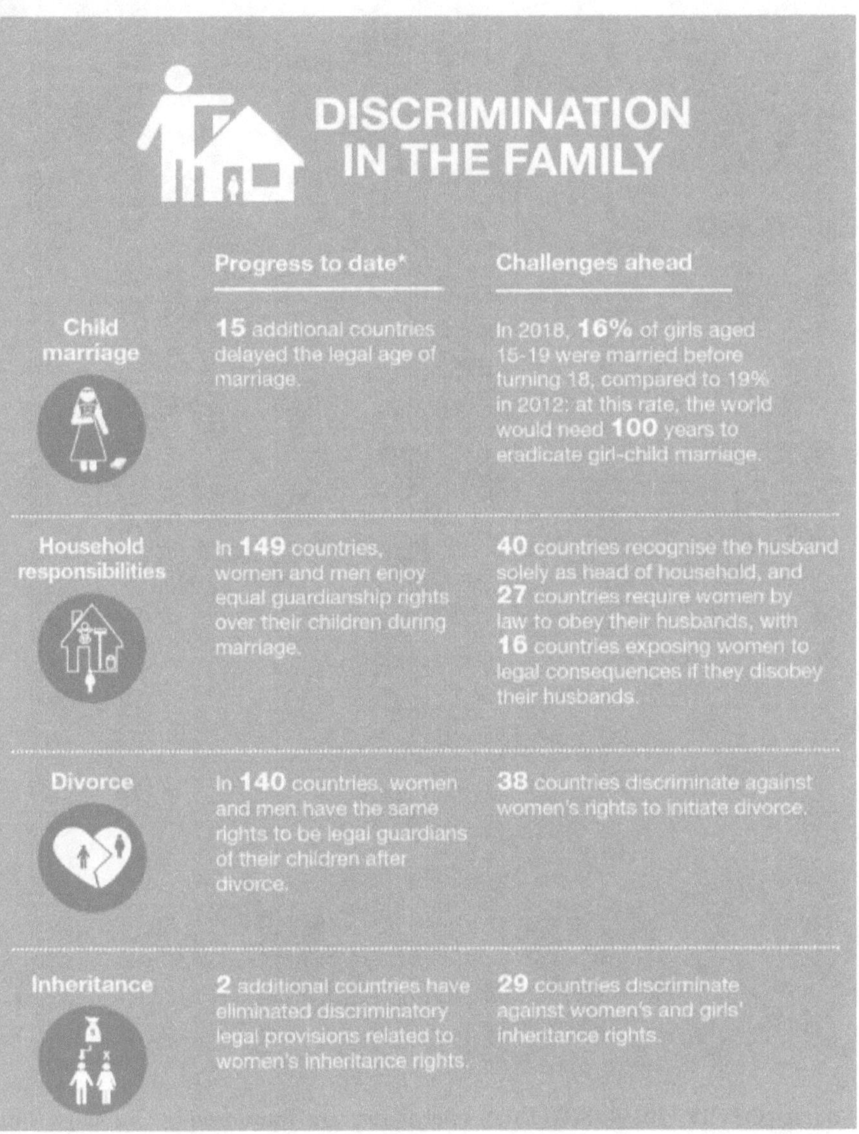

Source: OECD (2019), SIGI 2019 Global Report: Transforming Challenges into Opportunities, Social Institutions and Gender Index.

Source: OECD (2019), SIGI 2019 Global Report: Transforming Challenges into Opportunities, Social Institutions and Gender Index.

Source: OECD (2019), SIGI 2019 Global Report: Transforming Challenges into Opportunities, Social Institutions and Gender Index.

	Progress to date*	Challenges ahead
Citizenship rights 	**3** additional countries allowed women to transfer their nationality to a foreign spouse in the same way as men.	Women's rights to pass on their nationality are still restricted in **49** countries.
Political voice 	**10** additional countries introduced special measures to promote gender-balanced political representation.	**47%** of the world's population still believes that men make better political leaders than women.
Freedom of movement 	**2** countries removed discriminatory requirements regarding passport and ID applications.	In **125** countries, women are more likely than men to feel unsafe walking alone at night in the area where they live.
Access to justice	In **132** countries, women have the same legal rights as men to sue, provide testimony and hold office in the judiciary.	In **85** countries, women are more likely than men to express mistrust in the justice system.

Source: OECD (2019), SIGI 2019 Global Report: Transforming Challenges into Opportunities, Social Institutions and Gender Index.

Appendix 5: World Bank – data on gender (The Little Data Book on Gender)

Population (millions)	7,529.7
GNI, Atlas ($ billions)	78,399.7
GNI per capita, Atlas ($)	10,412.0
Population living below $1.90 a day (%)	9.9

	2000		2017	
	Female	Male	Female	Male
Education				
Net primary enrollment rate (%)	81	86	88	90
Net secondary enrollment rate (%)	53	57	66	66
Gross tertiary enrollment ratio (% of relevant age group)	19	19	40	36
Primary completion rate (% of relevant age group)	79	85	90	91
Progression to secondary school (%)	87	88	91	91
Lower secondary completion rate (% of relevant age group)	61	66	77	76
Gross tertiary graduation ratio (%)	..	..	..	..
Female share of graduates from STEM (%, tertiary)	..		..	
Youth literacy rate (% of population ages 15–24)	83	90	90	93
Health and related services				
Sex ratio at birth (male births per female births)	1.08		1.07	
Under-five mortality rate (per 1,000 live births)	75	79	37	41
Life expectancy at birth (years)	70	66	74	70
Contraceptive use, modern methods (% of women ages 15–49)	55		49	
Pregnant women receiving prenatal care (%)	69		86	
Births attended by skilled health staff (% of total)	63		80	
Maternal mortality ratio (per 100,000 live births)	341		216	
Women's share of population ages 15+ living with HIV (%)	50		52	
Prevalence of HIV (% ages 15–24)	0.6	0.3	0.4	0.2
Prevalence of smoking (% of adults)	11	44	6	35
Economic structure, participation, and access to resources				
Labor force participation rate (% of population ages 15+)	51	78	48[a]	75[a]
Labor force participation rate (% of ages 15–24)	43	61	34[a]	50[a]
Wage and salaried workers (% of employed ages 15+)	45	46	53[a]	52[a]
Vulnerable employment (% of employment)	54	50	46[a]	45[a]
Employment in agriculture (% of employed ages 15+)	40	40	28[a]	29[a]
Employment in industry (% of employed ages 15+)	18	23	17[a]	27[a]
Employment in service (% of employed ages 15+)	43	36	55[a]	45[a]
Women's share of part-time employment (% of total)	..		..	
Maternity leave (days paid)	..		..	
Women are able to work in the same industries as men	..		..	
Employment to population ratio (% ages 15+)	48	74	45[a]	71[a]
Employment to population ratio (% ages 15–24)	38	55	29[a]	44[a]
Firms with female participation in ownership (%)	..		35	
Firms with a female top manager (%)	..		19	
Children in employment (% of children ages 7–14)	..	..	..	..
Unemployment rate (% of labor force ages 15+)	6	5	5[a]	5[a]
Unemployment rate (% of labor force ages 15–24)	13	12	15[a]	12[a]
Internet users (%)	..	..	..	..
Account at a financial institution (% age 15+)	..	..	64	71
Mobile account (% age 15+)	..	..	3.4	5.5

Source: World Bank (2019). The Little Data Book on Gender 2019.

Appendix 6: Global trends in gender equality

Regional gender gaps: evolution in scores, 2006 – 2021 (World Economic Forum)

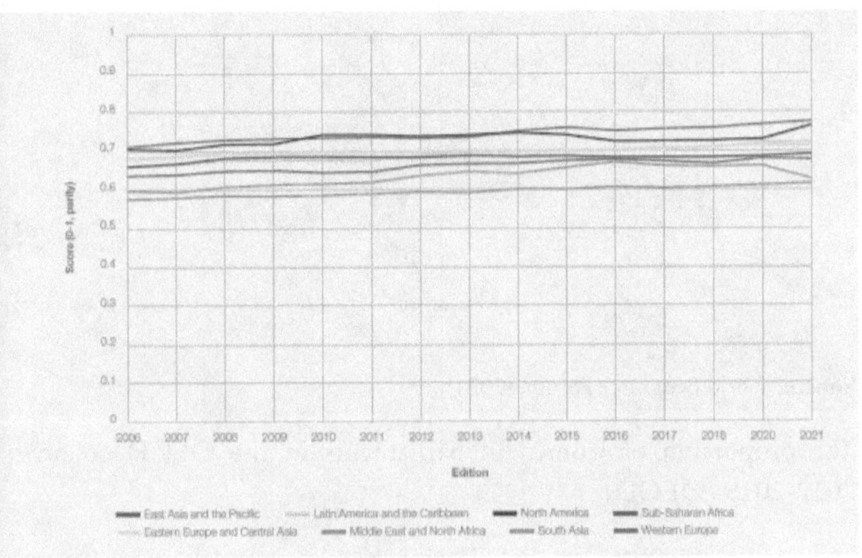

Source: World Economic Forum, (2021).

Change in Global Gender Gap sub-index performance by region (World Economic Forum, 2021)

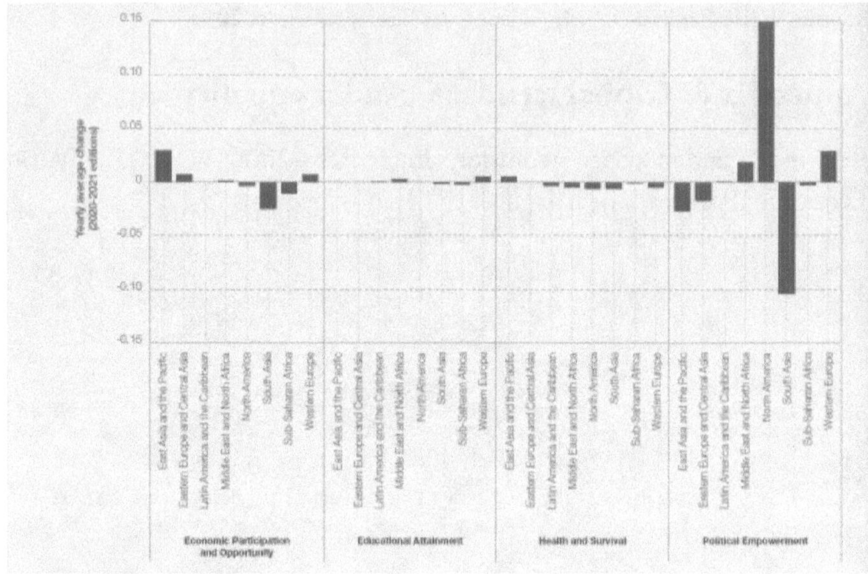

Source: World Economic Forum, (2021).

The proportion of women in parliaments in the OECD countries, 2012-2019 (OECD)

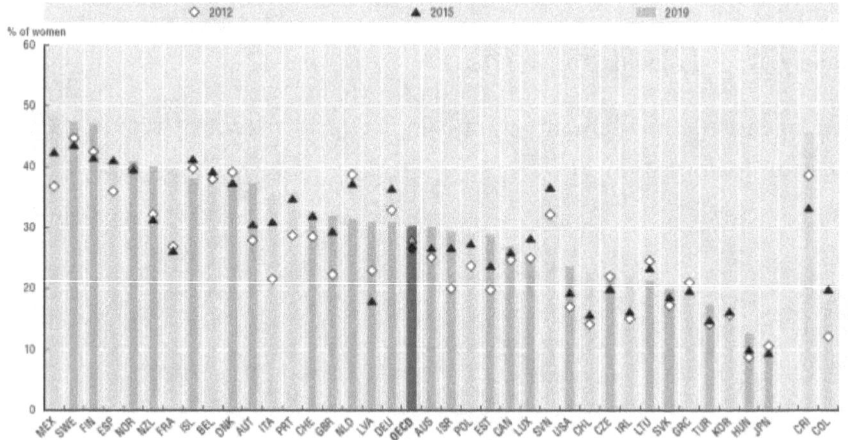

Source: Inter-Parliamentary Union (IPU) PARLINE (database), and IDEA Quota Project (database), Data for Finland for 2019 were provided by national authorities.

[1] Please note that the total population of the 129 countries reviewed in the report was around 3.5 billion, representing around half of the world population.

[2] https://www.unwomen.org/-/media/headquarters/attachments/sections/library/publications/2018/sdg-report-fact-sheet-global-en.pdf?la=en&vs=3554

[3] https://unstats.un.org/unsd/demographic-social/products/worldswomen/documents/WW2020_Infographics.pdf

Don't miss out!

Visit the website below and you can sign up to receive emails whenever Milos Kankaras publishes a new book. There's no charge and no obligation.

https://books2read.com/r/B-A-GHFU-BDWZB

BOOKS2READ

Connecting independent readers to independent writers.

Did you love *The Global State of Gender Equality: An Overview of Empirical Findings*? Then you should read *Domestic Violence: Effectiveness of Intervention Programs*[1] by Dr. Milos Kankaras!

[2]

Domestic violence was long ignored or underestimated policy topic. It was not until the last decade of the 20th century that most countries started focusing on this issue and introducing lawful protections against it in their legal systems. Increased attention to the problem resulted in a growing number of intervention programs aiming to prevent the occurrence or reoccurrence of various forms of domestic violence. Unfortunately, in the beginning, these interventions mainly relied on anecdotal accounts and untested assumptions. However, this is slowly changing in recent years, with an increasing number of programs using more robust empirical methods to evaluate their desired impacts.

---

1. https://books2read.com/u/md6kjX

2. https://books2read.com/u/md6kjX

Without valid and reliable data on the effectiveness of domestic violence interventions, we will not be able to introduce positive change in this area. That is why this book focuses on examining and evaluating existing empirical evidence from around the world on the effectiveness of interventions in the field of domestic violence. In other words, we try to answer "what works", i.e. what is known to be an effective intervention strategy against domestic violence, under which conditions, and for which outcomes.

Read more at https://oecd.academia.edu/MilošKankaraš.

Also by Milos Kankaras

Gender Equality
Policy and Research on Gender Equality: An Overview
The Global State of Gender Equality: An Overview of Empirical Findings
Violence Against Women and Girls: Effectiveness of Intervention Programs

About the Author

Dr Miloš Kankaraš is an experienced policy analyst, project manager and author with a rich track record in providing an empirical foundation for evidence-based public policy in international settings. He worked in academia before moving to some of the leading international organisations, where he examined issues ranging from education, skill development, social policy, working conditions, gender equality, quality of life, etc. Miloš published extensively in a variety of policy and research areas. He has an undergraduate degree in Psychology, graduate degrees in educational psychology and international social policy, and a PhD in the area of cross-cultural research.

www.ingramcontent.com/pod-product-compliance
Lightning Source LLC
Chambersburg PA
CBHW030811170726
47995CB00011B/469